THERE'S A REASON I LIKE SUNSETS

Roela Dhima

To first loves…

.

CONTENTS

ACKNOWLEDGMENTS

To my family and friends – thank you for
your unwavering encouragement and
support throughout this journey. There is
nobody I'd rather have by my side during
all of life's little moments.

To my inspiration – may the sunlight find
you even on the coldest of days.

Part I. The Rise

Moonlight Prayers

The moon, she listened, but did not ask
and so I never said your name,
but she was wise and always knew
for you were speaking to her, too

Firsts

The petals are still drying
from the flowers that you sent,
the verses that you wrote
still replaying in my head

Even the rain when it comes
feels as warm as the sun,
bringing memories of that day
when our journey had just begun

I think of ferries and tremble,
heartbeat speeding to a rush,
like in the ticket office one morning
that first time we touched

They say first times are special
and when I saw you I knew
that I'd forever be wishing
for all my firsts to be with you

There's A Reason I Like Sunsets

It's not the quiet certainty
that tomorrow will rise again
or the patterns in the sky
with no beginnings or ends

It's not the orange flames
that engulf the open blue
or the colors in the clouds
of pink and purple hues

There's a reason I like sunsets,
and it's because of you

It's the way the sun's glow
reminds me of your smile
lightening up my world
despite the countless miles

It's the warmth of the rays
blazing over the land
burning through my skin
as when you touched my hand

I stare into the depth
like my eyes meeting yours,
brown gaze upon brown,
a meeting of the souls

Darkness falls and I find
only more thoughts of you,
the sun leaves yet you remain,
you're the reason I like the moon

Permanent

I haven't written in a while,
it must be true what they say,
happiness rarely inspires,
pen is only put to paper
when there is sadness to convey

Rest assured,
that is not the case tonight
or yesterday, or tomorrow,
where your footprints have traveled,
through my mind, my heart, my soul,
only happiness can follow

For this reason, in this moment,
on this cold December night
as I'm missing your embrace,
I simply wanted to say
thank you
for the endless smile on my face

Game Day

Dressed in opposite gear,
hand in hand we walked,
a united front
representing different shades of blue

We bore different armor
and spoke different tongues
but through our eyes we said,
I'll always fight beside you

A Christmas Gift

You wrote to me on Christmas,
words I had heard before
from strangers and friends

You were a stranger, too

Yet, when you wrote
"Merry Christmas"
I read it as "I love you"

Insignificant

What is it? You ask
as I slide a small paper bag your way,
something small, I whisper,
insignificant,
I just saw it the other day.
You pick it up, unopened,
storing it away,
we both know it isn't the trinket inside
I give you
but my heart instead,
hoping you don't throw it away

No Doubt

If you ever doubt my love
let those thoughts be short and swift,
see yourself through my eyes and find
a blinding sky of green, the northern lights,
the world's rarest of gifts

If the distance seems endless,
my touch growing cold,
feel your skin through my hand
to understand why it's said
a person can feel like home

If you can't hear my words,
my voice too far away,
listen for your name in the wind
whispered from my lips in prayer
every night and every day

If in the dark your bed feels empty,
the uncertainty seeping through,
hold your head close to my chest,
in the quiet rhythm realize
my heart only beats for you

If you ever doubt my love
listen to the moon and see
how it calls out to the sun
like my soul to yours, saying
You're the better half of me

The Breakers

We walked slowly up the grand staircase
taking in the opulence around us,
the painted ceiling,
the gold paneling,
the crystal chandeliers,
discovering the riches of the gilded age
with each twist and turn
until the tour came to an end

Peeking back at the mansion
in the rearview mirror,
I smiled, feeling wealthier
than any who lived there before
as I held tightly to your hand

2.14

A call, a knock, a kiss,
red rose petals
grazing my skin,
lips touching lips.
You sit across
button left undone
your eyes teasing
with promises to come.
We speak in silence
of half hearts,
broken but true,
breaths mingling,
fast and slow,
souls merging from two.
Then, finally, words
long left unspoken
whispered in the dark
I love you

No Name

There's something about your name
when it settles on my tongue
flooding my mouth with honey
breathing life into my lungs

It flows through my body
streaming towards the heart,
a river meeting the ocean
an arrow finding its mark

It descends into the depth
merging with the soul
returning as a prayer
spoken from my core

It emerges from my lips,
a sacred vow, whispered quick,
an amen to the heavens,
my favorite word
[   ]

32

Another year gone, say some,
another day lived, say others,
but I didn't start counting
'til you

Humans, like puzzles,
remain unfinished
until they meet another,
the missing half of two

Thirty-two years of searching
and endless wishes
on candles and stars,
you finally came true

Morning Call

As daylight peeks through the window,
I open my eyes and smile,
feeling the flutters in my stomach,
the excitement rushing through,
knowing you'll call in an hour

The smell of coffee swirls in the air
luring me towards that first sip,
it hits my tongue, strong and sweet,
lingering long after, perhaps forever,
like the first taste of your lips

Perched on the kitchen counter,
holding my phone to my chest,
I glance at the clock and wait,
it reads 7:00 in the morning,
finally, my favorite time of day

Long Distance

Distance means nothing
when I would drink the ocean
drop by drop
to reach the depths of your soul

Angel Numbers

11:11, but I don't make a wish —
nothing in this world comes free,
I offer the universe a trade instead,
asking it to make you whole
in return for little parts of me

I offer my hands so you can feel
a healing touch upon your scars,
I offer my feet to keep you grounded,
to guide you through the darkness
under the moonlit stars

I offer my eyes to help you see
the sunlight through the trees,
I offer my time, my days, my years,
to add a happy ending
to your tragic memories

My heart, I cannot offer,
though it beats steady and true,
it isn't mine to give any longer,
it's always belonged to you

Too Far Gone

Sometimes when you ask me
why I seem nervous or cold,
I mumble an apology,
too afraid to speak the truth,
too tongue-tied to respond

How do I tell you
if I stare for too long
when I meet your gaze,
I start drowning in warm whiskey
so I quickly look away

How do I pretend
I'm not shivering
when your skin touches mine,
reducing me to ashes,
burning me up inside

How do I greet you
by getting lost in your kiss
when soon we'll say farewell
and knowing it feels like heaven
becomes a different kind of hell

So I'm sorry if sometimes
I seem nervous or cold,
I'm simply afraid
if I hold on for too long,
I'll never let you go

Flutter

There's a flutter in my chest
that sings when you're around,
lost for years in the silence
it roars now that it's been found.
At times I think you hear it
pulling you in with its song,
urging you to move closer
to the place where you belong.
When we finally embrace,
your heart upon my own,
it hums and trills and purrs
that it's finally home

Muddy Waters

I never liked brown
until I sat across your eyes
in a coffee shop one morning
where I suddenly realized,
thinking of all the colors,
I now wished to spend eternity
drowning in muddy waters

When I Say I'm Thinking About You

I'm thinking about your chest
and the way one side swells
slightly higher than the other
as if you have squeezed
too many things inside your heart,
yet I still want to lay my head there
and ask if it can make room for another
before it breaks apart

I'm thinking about the fortress
you build around yourself when you sleep,
tucking the blanket at your sides,
perhaps to keep the darkness
from lurking in your dreams.
As you lay there, too far to touch,
enveloped in your self-made cocoon,
I fall asleep waiting,
wishing for the day
I'll lay there with you

Happy Birthday

I know you'll say today
is just another day,
but it's my favorite day of the year.
It doesn't bring me gifts,
or flowers, or balloons,
it simply commemorates
one thing I hold dear

I won't blow out candles
but I'll make a wish for you,
for today, for tomorrow,
for when you're ninety-two,
for every year in between
my only wish will be
for you to feel truly happy,
as happy as you make me
(the happiest I've ever been)

Forsythias

I saw the forsythias today,
suddenly I felt you near,
the soil must be warm, you'd say,
a sign that spring is here

In that moment I wondered,
are people like flowers, too,
needing our souls touched by fire
before we can fully bloom?

Then I remembered last April,
in the rain where I met you,
the walls around my heart melted
and the forsythias grew

For Survival

Like water from a stream
you flow through me
replenishing a need.
A survival tool,
for ages necessary to man,
my body parched for life
until I drink again

Eclipse

You came suddenly one day,
your shadow slowly creeping in
until you covered everything,
leaving my world colored
with the essence of you.

Please stay forever.

I am a moon lover, you see,
and darkness never bothered me.

Through

There comes a time
the only path forward
is through the forest
where the dark trees tower

Step in, don't be afraid,
for just past the hedges
you'll find
there blooms a yellow flower

Soulmates

I called your name out to the wind
and heard my own
whispered back in the breeze

Even the universe cannot distinguish
where you end and I begin

Part II. The Fall

Forever

"I promise," you said
and I thought, "it must be true."
"I promise," you said
I replied, "I love you, too."
"I promise," you said
and then you left,
my last words unspoken,
"I'll always miss you."

A Past Life

There was a time I loved you
when flowers sprouted
from your lips,
there was a time I loved you
when fire burned
at your fingertips

There was a time I loved you
when copper sizzled
through your eyes,
there was a time I loved you
when clouds formed
by your sighs

There was a time
I loved you.
There was a time
you loved me, too.

Think of Me Sometimes

Someday,
when you are sitting on your porch
in a rocking chair
under the summer heat,
the only sound
the wood creaking beneath your feet,
I hope you think of me
and still hear my laughter
echo through the trees

Someday,
when you are driving home
from the grocery store,
you turn on the radio,
hear the music come on,
I hope you think of me
and smile when you remember
that it was my favorite song

Someday,
if the memory of us has faded,
our fate long ago decided
by God, or life, or luck,
I hope you think of me
out of the blue
and in that moment know
that somewhere, near or far,
I am always thinking of you

Rewrite

I imagine I'm an author
sometimes,
writing stories,
long, untold novels
or short, succinct rhymes

I think of your life,
the heroes, the villains,
the sad and happy times

My imagination taking over,
I put pen to paper to begin,
but I don't make any changes,
I just add myself in

Almost

Life plays tricks on us
treating us to a glimpse
of our deepest desires,
making us believe in *forever,*
waiting until it's almost in our grasp
before it dissolves this vision
like sand slipping through our fingers,
almost becoming *never*

Knight in Shining Armor

We spend our lives searching
for our knight in shining armor
until we realize
armor is hard to pierce through

I made a small dent
in the area around your heart
until I felt the scars forming,
my love bleeding out,
but it never reached you

63

The Cold War

I'm a lover, not a fighter
but I'll fight for my love,
I was born in winter, you see,
made to withstand the cold

With warmth as my armor
I can melt hearts of stone,
and if you are too tired to fight
I'll win this war alone

Should the next one come around
I'll fight that one and another,
until the sun shines once more
and we live in endless summer

Gift

I almost bought a gift today
and mailed it out like I used to,
wrapped in a pretty bow

If I never wrote my name inside,
would you think it was from me,
would you even care to know?

Maybe you'd almost call me,
as you used to do before,
or is there a different number,
another someone you'd rather call,
who now brings gifts to your door?

Daydreams

I like it when we talk about the future
and how pretty you think I'll look
dressed in white on our wedding day

I like to imagine the feel of the sand
as I sit under the sun, book in hand,
watching you fish out on the Bay

I like visions of warm summer days,
lawnmower going and peaches growing
and dogs barking while the children play

Tell me, love,
when you choose to go,
will the daydreams stay?

Poetry for Me

I read your poems from time to time
though I know the words by heart,
I even believe them sometimes,
the promises that we'd never be apart

Once proof of fate's unwavering will,
now wistful words and lessons learned,
I keep them stapled to my chest,
receipts of a love you have now returned

Shadow

My shadow walks with me today
getting bigger as the sun goes lower,
I wonder if it'll reach you by sunset
if I walk a little slower

It disappears in the night,
obscured from my view,
but I walk on in the darkness
hoping maybe tomorrow
it'll walk beside you

Familiar Strangers

We are strangers,
you and I,
but maybe one day,
years from now,
we'll meet.
My eyes will find yours
across a coffee shop
or a crowded street.
You'll nod
and I'll smile
but we'll both know
that's all we'll ever be.

Bittersweet

I woke up today,
I didn't think of you,
not right away.
It was unusual, unfamiliar,
an illusion that the danger had passed,
my body no longer under threat.
Then the memories came flooding back,
with them a bittersweet relief,
my heart torn between
wanting to let go but refusing to forget

Drowned by Love

You were a flower
and I,
who had never been given flowers before,
in my attempt to make you last forever,
placed you on the windowsill
and watered you everyday

By the time I realized
that water is poison
to flowers raised in the desert,
you had already withered away

Souvenir

What do you want me to bring back for you?
One of those Swiss Army knives, you said,
so I searched all the stores of Zurich
seeking the perfect one

I wish I hadn't looked so hard
to find the one you'd like,
I wish I'd picked a different knife
whose blades were not as sharp

I wish I had known then
the perfect gift I sought
would now sit fully lodged
inside my own heart

Different

I'm still the same person
but when I smile,
it doesn't quite reach my eyes anymore,
and when I laugh,
it isn't quite as loud as before,
when I hear a ring
I no longer run to pick up the phone,
and I still worry
but I don't call to ask if you've made it home

I'm still the same person
but when I speak,
there is conviction lacking in my tone,
and when I walk,
I don't stop to smell the flowers on my way home,
I still watch the sunset
but no longer feel the warmth in my bones,
and I still read poetry
but the words no longer speak to my soul

I'm still the same person,
I'm just …
a little less whole

7.17

There was a rainstorm today
like the day when we first spoke,
how funny life can be –
it rained when my heart soared
it rained when my heart broke

Maybe it was never meant to last,
maybe now we'll never know,
how funny life can be –
the same day I finally found you
is the day I let you go

No Heartbeat

How do you explain heartbreak to someone?
How do you explain that it doesn't happen all at once?
Instead, it happens slowly, crack by crack,
each piece held together by a slender string of hope
until one day the string finally snaps,
the pieces flying out trying to burst from our body
as if trying to find their home,
trying to find you...
and that's how we live for days, or months, or years,
with tiny shards pressed against our chest,
each with its own tiny heartbeat,
yelling out a name that no longer responds,
until each beat gives its final breath
falling back into the emptiness that was once our heart,
only they don't go back to their original place.
So, in the end, we are left walking around
with a distorted shape where our heart used to be
hiding behind a happy face

Shattered

Fragile, you used to call me,
and I'd laugh, finding it endearing,
not knowing you'd set out to prove
how easily I could break

But who is the broken one, I wonder,
the one who chose to leave
or the one who chose to stay?

Powerful

There's a sad kind of magic
in the way our hearts keep beating
for people who are no longer here,
in the way we are flooded
with shock and pain and grief
yet the flame never bends

It must be the fated irony of life
that love shows its true power
long after it ends

3AM

Like clockwork, my eyes drift open
in the middle of the night,
restlessness taking over,
my soul searching, seeking...

Your absence present in my mind
recalling all the little things
like your hand gently touching me
and how you always had trouble sleeping

Are you awake now, too,
your brain pumping with thoughts of us,
or am I just a forgotten promise
you never planned on keeping?

As darkness slowly turns to dawn,
my whispered pleas fill the air
drenching the pillow with unshed tears
through which my love lays seeping

Now what?

It was supposed to be you
who'd call me on the way home
asking if we need milk,
it was supposed to be you
who'd walk through the front door
and wouldn't make it far
before a boy with bright eyes
who is not so little anymore
jumped into your arms

It was supposed to be you
who'd sit across the table
praising me for a recipe
I had finally gotten right,
it was supposed to be you
who'd walk through the house
and turn off all the lights
before laying down next to me
and kissing me good night

How do I shed the weight of unlived days,
erase this perfect picture my mind drew,
how do I dim the light of hope
when it was supposed to be you?

36 Questions

"If I ask you these, we'll fall in love "
you didn't hesitate when you said yes,
the knowing look in your eyes
mirroring my own,
It is inevitable between us

Thinking back to that moment,
I long to ask you once more,
hoping to hear in your voice
the same answer as before,
It is inevitable between us

Peaches

Have you ever tried to cut through a peach?
The knife smoothly slicing through the skin
breaching the slippery sweetness within
but before reaching its beating heart
stopped by a barrier,
impenetrable to get through

If we are what we eat
then it makes perfect sense
why peaches are your favorite fruit

Snowflake

It was August when you kissed me
under the moon
at the corner of an ice cream shoppe

Now every summer I crave
honeyed lips
and the aftertaste of mint chocolate chip

Sugar Free

Sometimes when I miss you,
the cravings too large to contain,
I order your regular,
café au lait, oat milk, sugar-free caramel,
sighing as the sweetness pumps into my veins

Sip by sip, I fill the void,
my starving soul now on the mend,
in my delirium I close my eyes
and taste your lips
pretending it is not pretend

Port Jefferson

Do you remember the old man we met
in that restaurant on the water,
how we promised we'd be back
once the weather got warmer?

I think of him sometimes
as the seasons change, cold to hot,
wondering if he remembers us
even though you forgot

Strong Memory

In a year, or two, or thirty,
will I still remember the look in your eyes
the first time you saw me,
or the shape of your bottom lip
when you smiled against my skin?

Will I still feel the pangs of yearning
as I recount stories to my children
of a love that might have been?

Homeless

This feels like home, I thought,
when you wrapped yourself around me
to shield me from the ocean breeze

Now I roam the world on frozen bones,
homesick for a pair of arms
to which I no longer have the keys

Alternate Universe

There is another world,
somewhere between dreams and dawn,
where we end up together.

I can't wait to meet you there.

Fight or Flight

I clipped my wings
and left the sky
to live with my love on land

When war came knocking at the door
I turned around and watched you fly,
your sword gripped firmly in my hand

I Miss You

In my language we say, "më mungon"
which translates into, "you are missing from me"

Sometimes, when I lay awake at night,
unable to quench the restlessness in my soul,
I can almost hear the muffled whispers
echo through the empty chamber beneath my chest,
You are missing from me

115

Grateful

Sitting in the throes of wretched grief,
I am grateful for the pain
and the unfinished memories
I now get to keep.

It's proof we once existed,
It's proof our love was deep.

The Last Sunset

My book is almost finished,
the last chapter closed tonight
as I wrote my final poem
under the sunset's burning light

I stared at the horizon,
tried to hold it in my hand,
but that's the thing about sunsets,
they are incomparably magical
precisely because they end

ABOUT THE AUTHOR

"If you didn't document it, it didn't happen!"
The author took HR's golden rule and allowed
readers to experience the magic of falling in
love through her poetry.

Roela Dhima is the author behind "There's A
Reason I Like Sunsets." This is her debut
poetry book and marks a significant milestone
in the writer's career.

Anyone who's come across Roela, knows she is
the voice of reason and has a way of using
words in a way that pacifies the soul.

One of her favorite quotes, "Nobody chooses
evil because it is evil, they simply mistake it for
the happiness that they seek," embodies the
compassion with which she treats those around
her.

You can visit her online on Instagram
@reasonandrhymes.

www.ingramcontent.com/pod-product-compliance
Lightning Source LLC
Chambersburg PA
CBHW032037040426

42449CB00007B/931